What Is the Catholic Church?

by
Fr Stephen Wang

*All booklets are published thanks to the
generous support of the members of the
Catholic Truth Society*

Contents

Some important questions

Many people are puzzled by the idea of the Church. They may believe in God, and have faith in Jesus, and study the bible, and pray, and try to lead good lives. But they don't understand why we need a Church. It seems unnecessary. It seems like something that gets in the way of our relationship with God. And the Catholic Church, above all, can be a source of confusion or even of scandal. It is a large institution with a complicated history that insists on making great claims for itself. To many people these claims seem absurd. They ask themselves: "What has the Catholic Church got to do with Jesus Christ? What has this Church got to do with me and with my personal faith?"

This pamphlet will look at some of the claims that the Catholic Church makes, and show why the Catholic Church is so important for our lives as Christians. It does not explain every Catholic teaching; it just tries to answer some of the basic questions that people have about the Church. It shows that the Church is a gift from God, founded by Jesus Christ himself; that Jesus continues to teach us through his Church; that Jesus is present with us through his Church, especially in the sacraments, and above all in the sacrament of the Eucharist; and that the Catholic Church has a special place in history because it contains the fullness of all the gifts that Christ wants to give to the world.

Why do we need the Church?

Jesus Christ founded his Church

We can't talk about the Church without talking about God, and about his plans for us. Two thousand years ago God sent his only Son to us so that we could find peace with him and with each other, and share in his divine life. Jesus Christ, the son of Mary, who was born in Bethlehem, is the eternal Son of God. He became a human being like us, while remaining truly and completely divine. He came into the world that had been created through him. He lived among us, he taught and healed and forgave, he suffered and died and was raised to life again. Jesus Christ is the way of God; he is the truth about God and about ourselves; he is God's own life lived among us. He is the beginning and end of all our deepest longings and hopes, and of all the other things that we never dared to hope for. This is the mystery of Incarnation: Jesus Christ is truly God and truly human; he is God with us.

Many people wonder what it would have been like to know Jesus two thousand years ago, to walk with him, follow him, listen to him, touch him - God himself living with us. What is incredible is that we can be this close to him, as close as his first followers were. He did not leave us alone. Through the Church all the good things that he revealed to those who knew him are still given to us today. Through the Church Jesus Christ is still present in the world right now, God truly with us, just as surely and completely as he was two thousand years ago.

The mystery of the Church only makes sense because of the mystery of the Incarnation. We are creatures of flesh and blood, and God chose to reveal himself through the flesh and blood of Jesus. God respects the fact that we are physical beings, instead of trying to bypass it. He doesn't pretend we're spirits or angels. He uses visible, material things - people, places, objects - to tell us about deeper spiritual things.

God continues to use human beings to be the sign of his presence in the world, the means by which we can be united with him and with each other. Jesus did not leave an idea or a plan or a book or a letter about himself. He left a group of people, his Church, who would be his life and his body. This Church was united, visibly united - it was not just a hidden unity of feeling or hope. This Church was catholic, that is, universal - it was the means by which *all* people would come to know him. He chose twelve apostles to make disciples of all nations. He told them to hand on all that they had received from him, to hand on his revelation. He promised that he would give his Holy Spirit to the apostles - the Spirit of God; God's power and truth, God himself. He sent them out with this Spirit to proclaim the coming of God's kingdom - to baptize and to teach, to forgive sins and to unite all people. This Spirit would guide them and lead them into all truth.

The apostles and their successors would be continuing witnesses to Christ. They would speak in his name; whoever listened to them would be listening to Christ, whoever rejected them would be rejecting Christ. In this way the whole Church, led by the apostles, would be the continuing presence of Jesus Christ in the world. The Church spread out from Jerusalem; it lived, prayed, suffered, thought and wrote; it handed on the living Word of God that had been given to it.

The Catholic Church today

There is a danger of idealising this early Church, of pretending that there were trouble-free apostolic days when the Church didn't have any problems or disagreements. But the Church has always had problems. Its members have *always* fought and argued. Right from the start there have been times when the disagreements have become so bad that some people have left the Church and set themselves against it.

The staggering fact is that these arguments and splits have never stopped the Church being the one Church that

Christ founded. He didn't form the Church and make promises to it only to see it destroyed or broken apart. Even though different people have left it, it has always remained visible and united: the Church that Jesus Christ founded, the Church that he guides.

The life of this Church can be traced continuously through the last two thousand years of history right down to the Roman Catholic Church today. The same fullness of life and truth that was given to the apostles is still given to the Catholic Church today. This is the most important claim that the Catholic Church makes about itself. Christ's life and truth are not limited by the Catholic Church, but in it they are most clearly found and guaranteed. The Church that he founded continues to be his living presence in the world, to be the one body that he has formed - teaching in his name, forgiving in his name, giving new life in his name, uniting in his name.

Change and development in the Church

But the Catholic Church has obviously changed so much over the centuries, and many people find it difficult to see how this can be the *same* Church that Jesus founded. Are Catholics being a bit naïve? Why don't they just admit that this is a different faith and a different Church?

It must be said that many things *have* changed in the Catholic Church since the time of the first apostles: its members, its size, its customs, its languages, its devotions, its culture. Of course the Catholic Church has changed in many superficial ways, of course it looks different. Two thousand years is a long time in which things can happen, some of them stranger than others. Some of these changes are superficial, some are very deep.

The deeper changes are less distracting but more important. The Catholic Church says that its faith has never changed, yet it speaks about its faith in new ways; its beliefs have developed. These developments are the result of the Church having a deeper and deeper understanding of its one unchanging faith, and expressing it in new ways. We would expect this of a living Church, one which doesn't remain stuck in the past, one which is the living presence of Christ in the world.

The love of the Church for Christ is constant, but this love deepens with time and experience. Over the years the Church has realised the enormous and sometimes painful implications of this love. In their daily lives individual Catholics try to live out their faith in fuller and more realistic ways. They constantly struggle simply to remain faithful, and this faithfulness changes lives and helps the whole Church to remain faithful.

The important developments that have taken place in the Catholic Church are not signs of failure or faithlessness (even though Catholics *have* failed and been faithless). These developments are the inevitable results of keeping faith in difficult, challenging and changing situations. They are not embarrassing compromises, but vital signs of the renewing power of the Holy Spirit at work in the Church. At each moment the Church has to work out how to live and communicate its one, unchanging love - Jesus Christ. At this level, the deepest level of what the Church is and what it is doing, the Church has not changed one bit. Nothing can be added to the revelation that Jesus gave to his apostles, nothing can be taken away.

Through all the changes, the heart of being a Catholic now is exactly the same as it was in 40AD. The Catholic Church today, in a direct and historical and visible line, is the same Church as the Church of the first apostles. Jesus Christ is the same today as he was yesterday and as he will be forever. Christian lives of prayer and love and sacrifice, lived in the faith of the Church, are at heart the same now as they always have been.

The problem of sin

Many people are sympathetic to the theory of the Catholic Church, but they are put off by the people who actually belong to it. They know from experience or from history that the Catholic Church is full of sinners; and they are shocked and sometimes scandalised that bad people come to church and pray and call themselves Catholics. Isn't this hypocritical? Does it not prove that the Catholic Church is not all it claims to be?

Catholics do not believe that the Church is faultless. In every generation, including our own, individual Catholics have done terrible wrongs, by themselves and in the name of the Church. This fact should sadden us, as all sin should sadden us, but it shouldn't surprise us. God could have formed a pure Church; he could have miraculously ensured that all Catholics acted perfectly, or excluded all sinners from his Church. But he didn't. He chose to build his holy Church out of sinful human beings, out of men and women who had betrayed and disowned him, out of people he knew would fail to believe and love him.

This is yet another consequence of the Incarnation. God is not a magician; he hasn't pulled a beautiful Church out of a hat and forgotten about human beings. He uses them, despite their faults, and transforms them in the process. He sent his Son into the heart of the world, and he uses the broken hearts of men and women to be his Church.

Bad Catholics are not being hypocritical by staying in the Church. Catholics realise that they can be sinful and this is why they stay in the Church - they need the grace and forgiveness given through the Church to help them change.

This doesn't excuse the turning away from God and from each other that we call sin. Sin is always wrong, and God always wants us to turn from sin and turn to him. But it does mean that sin has no power over God's plans.

Despite the cruelty, unfaithfulness and hypocrisy of individuals in every generation, the Catholic Church has always remained faithful to Christ, because Christ has always remained faithful to it. The Church always needs to be purified and renewed, but it is still always holy because of the holiness of Christ. This is the wonder of the Church, that God chose to show the glory of Jesus Christ through sinful human beings, so that his power and strength could be seen working through human weakness.

Holiness and the saints

After spending so much time thinking about sin, it's important to think about holiness. The Catholic Church is a Church of sinners because it is a Church *for* sinners, a Church to make us saints. Christ wants us to share his own life, to love perfectly in union with him, and to be his witnesses in the world - he wants us to be holy.

The end of holiness is to see God face to face in heaven, to be wrapped up in his joy and happiness forever in the company of all the angels and saints. The beginning of holiness is our present life of faith: trying to persevere in doing God's will, trying to hope, to love and to start again when we fail. Without Christ all these efforts would be difficult and ultimately futile. With Christ, in faith, our good thoughts, words and actions, however small, are given an infinite value. Our prayers, joys and sufferings become his, and his wisdom, power, holiness and freedom become ours.

The Church has many beginners; it also has many saints. The saints are not those people who have arrived at the end, but those who have seen what the beginning is really about. They are not a strange group of people different from ourselves; they are who we could be, who we should be. Every Catholic, simply by being a member of the Church, shares in the invaluable gifts of faith and hope and love. All these gifts reflect the one gift of being united with Christ in the Church. The saints are those people who have realised what this means, not just in their minds but in their hearts and their whole lives. They help us to see the essential holiness of the Church - the life of Christ in the Church - the source of their own holiness.

No two saints are alike, because each one reflects a different aspect of Christ's love in his or her own particular way. But they all have something in common: they love God with all their strength; they care for others more than for themselves; they forgive when they are wronged; they give all that they have to give; they fight against evil and injustice; they patiently accept the sufferings that God sends them - happy to share in the suffering of Christ; they try never to do anything that they know to be wrong; they believe what the Church teaches; they pray unceasingly, because they know that prayer is the life of God in them; they offer all that they have to God for his praise and glory. Everything is done in union with Christ and with the whole Church.

The saints long to be in heaven, because they know that heaven is, ultimately, what life is about. They know that God has promised us so much more than happiness in this life. But they also long to start living heaven on earth, to bring Christ's love and truth to the world. The saints, those who care most about heaven, are also those who care most about this world, because they can get on with God's work without worrying about themselves. Their hope for the future does not distract them from loving God in the nitty-gritty of the present.

The saints continue to do God's work after death - he uses them in heaven as he used them on earth. We pray to the saints and to the holy angels, we ask them to pray for us, because death is not a barrier but a bridge for those who love one another in Christ. We especially ask them to pray for the holy souls in purgatory, those people who have died but who are still being prepared for heaven. These people are already with God, yet they need our prayers to help them through the wonderful but painful process of learning to love and to forgive perfectly.

This is the whole Church, the Church of heaven, purgatory and earth, the body of those who are united with Jesus Christ.

How does Christ teach us through the Church today?

The New Testament and the Church

The Church gives us Christ's life in many ways. One way is by teaching. When we think of the teaching of Jesus, the first thing we usually think of is the Bible, and especially the New Testament. We look to the New Testament to discover what Jesus said and did; we look to it for Christian truth and moral guidance. But it's important to understand where the New Testament comes from, and why we need the Church if we are going to trust the Bible.

The first Christians, gathered around the apostles and their disciples, learnt and lived their faith in the Church. They were united with Christ and with each other. These Christians did not have a New Testament. The only holy scriptures they had were those that we call the Old Testament which they inherited from the Jews. The Church's knowledge of Jesus Christ was not written down but was handed on in its traditions and teaching and worship.

As time passed the many spoken accounts of the life and teaching of Christ were written down - sometimes in short records, sometimes in letters, eventually in longer accounts called gospels. Some of the writings that were written by about the end of the first century soon came to be regarded as scripture, and were read throughout the Church together with the Old Testament. This happened because the Church, under the authority of the apostles and their successors, accepted them and recognised that they were inspired by God.

There were doubts, however, about which writings should be included in this collection. These doubts went on for many generations. Eventually, throughout the fourth century, various Councils of bishops of the Church decided which Christian writings were inspired and authoritative. The 'books' included in this list form what we now call the New Testament, which together with the Jewish scriptures makes up the whole Bible. The Catholic Church has kept to this list since the end of the fourth century, even though some Christian groups have rejected certain books at different stages since then. This same Church has constantly been defending and interpreting the Bible and helping people to understand it more fully.

The vital questions are not 'Do we trust the Bible? Is it true?' but 'Do we trust this Church? Is it Christ's Church?' The New Testament is only as important as the Church that it describes, as the Church that lived and wrote and collected it, as the Church that today still reads and interprets it. The New Testament is the book of the

Church, written by the apostles of the Church and their companions under the inspiration of God's Spirit. We will only love and trust the New Testament fully if we love and trust the Church. We will only really trust that Christ guides this Church of the past if we trust the Church in that past and in every age, including our own.

It's not obvious that the Bible we have is important. Many other books speak about God. Many other books, some as old as the writings of the New Testament, speak about Jesus. For many centuries Christians have believed that the Bible was inspired by God because the Catholic Church taught this, because it was the book of the Church. It would be strange to believe in the Bible without believing in the Church that wrote it and approved it and has been nourished by it throughout the centuries.

Christian teaching

Jesus did not leave us alone. Catholics believe that he continues to love and teach and unite his people through the Catholic Church. Many Christian communities are aware of the different ways in which we come to know him - through the Bible, through the lives of Christian men and women, through the inspiration of God in our hearts and minds, through the teaching of Christian leaders. But we are given even more than this. The Catholic Church claims that it can speak the truth, in Jesus' name. It speaks and teaches with authority, and says that people have a duty to listen to it. It makes claims on all people, as Jesus did, and not only on those who are attracted or attached to it.

Jesus *spoke* with authority and *taught* his followers: words are important, truth is important. It matters what we believe. It matters what we say about God and what he says to us. If we're careless about words and throw ourselves idealistically into living and loving we're likely to come unstuck. Our living and loving will probably become distorted or exhausted no matter how selfless we try to be. We need to hear God's living and guiding voice today, the *same* voice that Jesus' disciples heard. It's not enough to trust our feelings about what is right. It's not even enough to trust the Bible - we can fool ourselves too easily and twist its meanings to suit ourselves. God knows this only too well, and he has given us a way of hearing his living, teaching voice today, through the teaching of the Catholic Church.

Truth and reason

The Catholic Church teaches. This doesn't conflict with the fact that people have a duty as well as a desire to think and reason. We must honour God by using our God-given minds and hearts properly, and we must be satisfied that something is not unreasonable or prejudiced. One of the important functions of our reason, however, is to know its own limitations, to know when it needs to listen and pause and wonder. If we have been touched in some small way by Christ we will stop at nothing to discover who he is and how we can know him. Driven by this touch of mystery and wonder we will expect the truth about God to be greater than our expectations, to be challenging, shocking, frightening, awe-inspiring - not to be unreasonable, but to be beyond reason, to be more than our minds can grasp.

This is why Catholics believe what the Church teaches - they want to trust what God has told us about himself, to *trust* him, rather than just what they happen to think or understand unaided. Catholics are not stupidly submissive, but they are aware of what they can and what they cannot find out by themselves. They trust their Church because they trust Christ, and because through it they hear his living voice. Catholics know that the Church's teaching will not always be easy to accept, because the truth about God is sometimes discomforting. Faced with God's beauty and kindness we become aware of our own sinfulness, and this is painful and humiliating. We become aware of the demands that he makes on us as well as the wonderful things that he gives us.

If we follow the teaching of the Church we are bound to follow all God's commandments, and not just those that we happen to agree with; we have to accept the Church's whole faith and not just those beliefs that we find attractive or comprehensible or 'relevant'; we have to do things that we would rather avoid; we have to make sacrifices; we have to stand up to injustice and oppression in the world when we'd rather not; we have to stop pretending that we are already good and get on with the difficult business of actually trying to be good. But the comforts and rewards of listening to the Church far outweigh the difficulties. Nothing could be more precious than God's own life, his voice, his kindness - given to us through the Church.

The Pope and the Bishops

Many different people are responsible for teaching in the Catholic Church - not least parents and school teachers. One clear way that we hear God's voice throughout the whole Church today - teaching, challenging, correcting, encouraging - is through the Catholic bishops who are united with the Bishop of Rome, the Pope. Christ chose twelve apostles and sent them out with authority to baptize, teach, forgive and unite all people. This great plan for the world did not die when these first apostles died. Their successors have the same authority as themselves; they continue to be Christ's apostles.

The Catholic bishops united with the Pope are the apostles' successors. They are responsible for preaching and teaching, celebrating the sacraments, and uniting and governing the Church. Despite their different traditions, which enrich the variety and expression of Christian life, they all believe and teach the same Catholic faith. The bishops are not just messengers or symbols of Christ - they are one way of his being present in the midst of the Church and the world, in such a way that whoever listens to them is listening to Christ, and whoever despises them despises Christ. He is present in many ways in the world today. He is not limited by his Church. But it is above all through the bishops that he guides the Church and keeps it faithful to his teaching.

The Pope is the centre of unity of the Catholic bishops. Because of him we can see and understand the unity of the whole Church. Jesus Christ is the head of the Church; the Church is one body because it is united in him. Christ gave the Church a way of seeing and preserving that unity which he valued so much. He sent out all his apostles with authority and power, but he gave Peter a special role. Peter was to be the rock on which his Church was built. Peter was to have the particular job of guiding and teaching and feeding all Christ's followers, of confirming and strengthening their faith. Peter was to be the visible head around which the Church would be united, the foundation of visible unity.

Peter's role was not to last only a few years, and then come to an end: like the authority of the apostles, his role has been an essential part of the Church in every generation. The Church in every age, including our own, needs to be united through a visible head of unity, otherwise Christ would have no visible Church, but only thousands of separated communities. Just as Christ united and guided the early Church through Peter, he continues to guide and unite his Catholic Church through Peter's successor, the Pope, who has the same unique role that Peter had. Without Peter, Christ's promise of truth and unity would be weak and vague. With Peter, Christ's promises are clear and visible and impossible to ignore.

Infallibility

The bishops united with the Pope teach and feed and unite the Church all the time, but they do so in a special way through their infallible teaching. This teaching is at the heart of the Catholic faith. It is about beliefs and morals that are so clearly a part of the Church's faith that to reject them would be to reject the Church itself. In these matters the Catholic Church cannot be in error.

The infallibility of the Church is usually expressed in the constant and common teaching of all the bishops. It is sometimes expressed when the bishops meet in an ecumenical council, or when the Pope decides after consulting the bishops that a belief must be held by the whole Church. On these rare occasions, Christ's Spirit helps the Pope and the bishops to remain faithful and to be sure about the truth.

Catholics believe all the infallible doctrines that the Church believes, even the ones that confuse or unsettle them. In asking people to believe, the Church is doing no more than Jesus did. He often told people things that they did not like or understand. He accepted that some people who could not accept his words might leave him - and many did leave.

It's obvious from experience that Christians can have fundamental disagreements about what to believe and about how to live, about doctrine and morality. We need some trustworthy way of knowing the revelation that Jesus Christ gave to the Catholic Church. At certain times Jesus cuts through these disagreements and tells us quite plainly what to believe through his Church. This clarity doesn't belittle the mystery or wonder of faith, it heightens it - it stops us substituting our own individual opinions and squabbles for the amazing mysteries of faith which the Church treasures.

The infallibility of the Church is the infallibility of Christ; it is the fact that he is always faithful to his Church. The infallibility of the Pope and bishops is one way that we come to see something that the Church has known all along about Christ. This belief may be put in new words or phrases, but it is not a new belief, not new revelation. The Church constantly finds new ways of expressing its faith; it is always seeing its one true treasure in a dazzling new light.

Why do we need the Sacraments?

The sacraments

The sacraments are sacred signs through which Christ gives his divine life to us. Through them we worship God, he shows his love to us, and his work of making us holy is carried out.

We need these visible signs. We are not airy, ethereal beings: we are physical and spiritual beings with thoughts and feelings, with bodies, minds and hearts. God has shown his divine love to the world through the humanity of Jesus Christ, through his body, his mind and his heart. Who could have imagined, if they had not known Christ, that Almighty God loves us with such intimacy and tenderness, or with such ferocity and passion, or with such humility and sacrifice? The eternal Son of God, God himself, did not remain distant and hidden, he became human - someone whom we could hear, whom we could see with our own eyes, whom we could touch with our own hands. Two thousand years later we are not just left with memories or feelings or ideas about Christ - we can see him and hear him and touch him because of his presence in the sacraments.

In *baptism*, through water and the baptismal words, Christ himself cleanses our sinfulness and makes us members of his body, the Church. In *confirmation*, the bishop anoints us with holy oil, and Christ himself strengthens us and gives us the gifts of his Holy Spirit. At *confession*, (*the sacrament of penance, of reconciliation*), through the words of absolution spoken by the priest, Christ himself forgives our sins. In *marriage*, through their public promises of love, Christ binds together husband and wife in a lifelong union. In the *sacrament of orders*, through the bishop, Christ ordains particular members of the Church to share in a special way in his priesthood. In *the sacrament of the sick*, through anointing with holy oil, Christ gives new strength and hope to the sick and dying.

In the greatest sacrament, *the sacrament of the Eucharist, the Mass*, Christ does not just give us his gifts, he gives us himself.

Christ's real presence in the Mass

Catholics go to church at least every Sunday to celebrate the sacrament of the Eucharist, the Mass. They gather together as God's holy people, to pray together, to be nourished by God's Word as it is read from the Holy Scriptures and explained in the homily, and to unite themselves in the offering of the Eucharistic Sacrifice that is offered by the priest.

Jesus told his disciples that unless they ate his flesh and drank his blood they would not have life in them. He promised that whoever ate his flesh and drank his blood would be united with him, and would be raised up by him on the last day. At the Last Supper Jesus gave his followers his body to eat and his blood to drink under the appearances of bread and wine. He told them to repeat what he was doing.

These are shocking and baffling promises. Jesus' followers were shocked by what he said, and some were so shocked that they left him. This teaching about his flesh and blood became the line which divided his true followers from his false ones. His twelve disciples stayed with him - not because they understood, or because they were less shocked, but because they believed what he said and they knew that there was no-one else worth believing in. Catholics believe what Jesus said, and they also believe that these promises that he made are kept even in our own time. Like his one Church, and his teaching, the gifts of his body and blood are not confined to the past; they are not dead memories.

In the Mass, the memorial of the Last Supper, Christ changes bread and wine into his body and blood. Jesus Christ, God himself, truly human, becomes present in the world in front of our eyes. Under the appearances of bread and wine he is as truly present as he was two thousand years ago. By eating his body and drinking his blood we are perfectly united with him and with each other; we are made one with him and with each other in our bodies, our minds and our hearts. This is a foretaste of heaven, because it is the same Christ who now lives in heaven who is united with us in this Holy Communion. By having a taste of heaven in this life we are driven and helped to be saints, to start living heaven on earth.

Catholics have not invented strange beliefs about Christ's real presence; they simply do and believe what he told them to do and believe. Every single gift and grace that Christ gave to those who knew him he gives to us now through the Church. He loves us so much that he cannot bear to give us anything less than what he gave to his first followers. He cares for us so much that he gives us his living word through the Catholic Church; he unites us in his visible body, the Church; and he gives us his body and blood, his humanity and divinity, his very self, really and truly present in the Mass.

There is even more: he stays with us in this way. Christ's body and blood are reserved after Mass, so that the sick and the dying may be strengthened by receiving communion at any time. He is really present in this 'blessed sacrament' in the tabernacles of Catholic Churches throughout the world. With such humility and hidden power, he is continually present with us, able to accept our prayers of praise and sorrow, of thanks and hope.

Unity of faith in the Mass

The Mass is the sacrament of Christ's presence because it is the celebration of the Church's unity in him. Our unity with Christ and with each other in Holy

Communion strengthens and fulfils the same unity that we already have with him and with each other in the faith of the Church. There is only one Christ, only one unity. We express this unity with him through lives of faith, hope and love. This is why if we are refusing to love someone or to love God, through serious sin, we cannot receive Holy Communion - we cannot pretend that we truly love Christ or the Church. We must first ask for forgiveness and promise to love again by going to the sacrament of confession.

This is also why most Christians in Britain who are not Catholic cannot normally receive Holy Communion if they go to Mass (Orthodox Christians are an exception because of their special bonds with the Catholic Church). This can seem unwelcoming and unkind. It's certainly painful and difficult to live with - but it comes from the fact that the Catholic Church will not allow itself to offer a dishonest welcome or a misleading kindness. Union with Christ in Holy Communion at the Eucharist cannot usually be separated from union with him in the faith of the Catholic Church. The gift of the Eucharist and the gift of the Church are two aspects of the same thing. However close other Christians are to Christ and to the Catholic Church (and they can be very close indeed), they are still cut off in some way from the unity of the Catholic Church, and therefore they are normally cut off from communion in its celebration of the Eucharist. To share in

Holy Communion would not be an honest reflection of our Christian faith, which at present is not fully shared.

The sacrifice of the Cross

The Mass is the sacrament of Christ's presence because it is his sacrifice. He showed how much he loved us by suffering and dying in agony on a cross for us. This horrific death so many years ago might not seem to have anything to do with God's love. But it has got everything to do with God's love. Jesus Christ, the Son of God, could have run away from suffering and death and avoided the consequences of being good in an evil world. He could have said 'No,' like we all do, and taken the easy way out. Instead, he freely chose to keep loving, to keep seeking justice and truth. He kept on doing what he knew to be right, even though he knew that it would lead to his death. He gave everything that he had in perfect obedience to his Father's will and out of love for each one of us. Because of this he was raised from the dead - he has destroyed death and restored life.

This is the sacrifice of Calvary, the sacrifice of our salvation. Through this our sins are forgiven and we are raised to new life with Christ, raised to God's own life. The forgiveness of sins is not a small matter which only concerns religious people: it is the defeat of the evil that causes all the terrible violence and loneliness and hatred and suffering in the world. This has been accomplished once and for all, but it is only slowly being realised.

There is nothing in the world more important than this sacrifice - the whole of Christ's life looked forward to his suffering, death and resurrection. All his words and actions were just brief glimpses into the perfect love that he showed for us on the cross. We are all called to imitate this love and therefore to share in Christ's sacrifice - this is our share in his priesthood. We do this by receiving the sacraments, by living lives of praise, thanks and prayer, lives of holiness, self-denial and love. We do this especially by offering the sacrifice of the Mass.

The sacrifice of the Mass

There is only one sacrifice of Calvary: it cannot be repeated. This sacrifice is perfect: it cannot be added to. But it is not just a memory of a past event. At the Last Supper Jesus made this one perfect offering of himself *before* he died. He gave his body and blood to his disciples. He promised that whenever they did this in his memory they would receive his body *broken for them* and his blood *shed for them* - his sacrifice would become real and effective and present before them.

This is what happens every time the Mass is celebrated. At Mass, Christ's loving sacrifice is not merely remembered; it is made present to us and offered in front of our eyes. It is not a repetition or an addition. God has given us a way of really being witnesses to our salvation, of being caught up in this unique and perfect offering.

At Mass God enables us truly to be with Christ in his life, in his suffering, in his death, and in his glorious resurrection. We share everything that he went through - we receive his love, hear his words, comfort him in his sorrow, stand by him with his mother at the foot of the cross, and we are united with him and with each other as he is taken up to the glory of his Father. And just as we are present to Christ, he is present to us. Through his intimacy in the Mass he takes possession of every part of our being, he enters every moment of our lives; we are made into his image - if we allow him.

The sacrifice of the Mass is the same sacrifice as the sacrifice of the cross. This is why the Mass is the source and summit of our lives, the beginning and end of all that we do. The beginning of all that we do is the love that Christ has shown us on the cross, which is re-presented at the Mass - without this love all our loving efforts would be wasted. The end of all that we do is our union with him and with each other, which is experienced at the Mass - without this union all that we do would ultimately be meaningless.

The Mass is the centre of our lives - it is Christ's love for us and our union with him; it is our salvation. It is called a sacrament because it is our salvation given to us in human signs. We need faith to see the reality of the Mass. But it is the same salvation which we hope to possess in heaven, when there will be no need for faith and signs, when we will see God as he really is.

How does the Catholic Church relate to other Christian communities?

Other Christian communities

There are many different Christian denominations in Britain today - Anglican, Methodist, Baptist, United Reformed, Quaker, Pentecostal, house communities, and many others. These denominations - as well as the Orthodox churches, which have a special closeness with the Catholic Church - have such different origins, beliefs and traditions that it's unfair to classify them together, even though this is sometimes unavoidable.

It is sometimes assumed that because Catholics believe in the importance and uniqueness of the Catholic Church, they dismiss these other Christian communities. This is not at all true. The Catholic Church has *always* known that the beliefs and practices of non-Catholic communities can have enormous value. They share many gifts with the Catholic Church: they trust in the Bible as a guide to faith and life; they foster Christian lives of faith and hope, of love and devotion, and of prayer and sacrifice; they search for peace and justice; they have various Christian ministries; many celebrate Christ's death and resurrection by remembering the Last Supper; many celebrate the sacrament of baptism through which their members share in Christ's divine life. Christ unites these communities with each other and with the Catholic Church in different ways.

The most important question is not: 'Are these other denominations good and valuable?' Of course they are; we see their goodness in many ways, not least in the holy lives that so many of their members lead. Through their faith many people have come to know Christ, to be united with him, and to share in the salvation that he brings. Through their love Christ is actively present in the world. The most important question to ask is: 'Where can we be most sure of Christ's presence in the world today? Where can his love and truth be found most fully?'

Within the Catholic Church

We can be most sure of the presence of Jesus Christ in his one Catholic Church, the Church that he founded to be his life in the world. Only in the Catholic Church can we be confident that we share in all the gifts that Christ wishes to give us. Within the Catholic Church anything good or true is balanced by numerous other good and true things, by *all* that Jesus has revealed. Nothing is taken on its own. Everything - great or small, serious or trivial - is held together by the full and incomprehensible gift of Christ to his Church. Every good thing is seen in its proper context, and beliefs that might seem distant or opposed take on a new and truer light beside each other.

The silent prayer of countless contemplative monks and nuns is shared with the social and political and missionary activity of others. The faith of illiterate peasants is shared by sophisticated scholars. The informal, spontaneous worship of the charismatic movement is offered in union with the solemn prayer of the Latin Mass. Poverty, which has a rightful place, is honoured and respected along with luxury, which also has a rightful place; fasting with feasting, celibacy with sex, faith with good works, grace with nature, variety with unity, justice with mercy, the human with the divine. It's no surprise that the Catholic Church is often accused of contradictory faults at the same time - of being both superstitious and over-rational; of being both too political and too spiritual.

Despite the faults and failures of countless Catholics, the whole Catholic faith forms a harmony. Every good thing is praised and valued somewhere in the Catholic Church, but seen as part of the whole. This great variety never slips into anarchy, into people believing and doing just what they like, because it all comes from the Church's unity of faith and hope and love - it all comes from Christ.

Outside the Catholic Church

When something good or true is lived outside the Catholic Church it becomes separated in some way from the whole, and in the process it risks being

misunderstood. These separations from the Catholic
Church, such as those that happened at the Reformation,
were caused by the sin and faithlessness of a good many
people, including Catholics. Different people, shocked by
the corruption of certain Catholics, or by what seemed to
them to be the Church's lack of faith, chose to live their
Christian faith outside the unity of the Catholic Church -
even though they kept many of its beliefs and practices.
Other Christian groups have newly formed and started
with beliefs and practices which, unknown to them,
already existed in the Catholic Church.

For many different reasons these separated Christian
communities, perhaps without realising it, have accepted
parts of a very large gift. They have accepted things that
are true and good, but in the process they have become cut
off from that full visible unity which Christ wants for his
Church. They have risked losing touch with some of the
other gifts that Christ entrusted to the Catholic Church.

For example: nearly all Christians believe in the Bible
as God's inspired and holy word - but not all accept the
authority of the Church which has constantly recognised
and guarded the authority of this Bible. Many
communities accept the sacrament of baptism which
Jesus gave to the Church for the forgiveness of sins - but
they do not always appreciate the sacrament of
confession which he also gave to the Church to renew
this forgiveness.

Some communities celebrate Christ's death and resurrection by remembering the Last Supper - but do not necessarily believe in his real presence and sacrifice at this Supper. Many Christians accept some of their beliefs or creeds on the teaching authority of Catholic bishops in the past - but do not accept the authority of Catholic bishops in the present.

The fullness of the Catholic Church

The different denominations live these beliefs away from their fullest context and because of this they are in danger of being distorted. The different Christian communities, partly because of the faults of Catholics, have not realised that their own true beliefs are a fundamental part of the Catholic faith. Perhaps they are more hidden than they should be, and need drawing out. Perhaps they are quieter than they could be, and need shouting about. But the effectiveness of the gifts which Christ has given to these communities comes from the fullness of grace and truth which he has given to his Catholic Church. Only the Catholic Church possesses *all* the good things that Christ has given to help us to share in his salvation.

These communities live their Christian lives with great faithfulness, self-sacrifice and humility. Most of them do not claim to represent the One Church of Christ, nor do they claim to speak infallibly in his name. When they have to puzzle over problems which constantly face all Christians - problems about *what* to believe (about doctrine), about *how* to believe (about worship and morals), and about *why* to believe (about authority) - they come to different conclusions. They recognise that their conclusions do not come with the force of Christ's word or with the assurance of his Holy Spirit. Many of their members would regard such force or assurance as dangerous and arrogant in matters to do with Christian faith, and this is why they might be wary of Catholic authority.

The Catholic Church *would* be dangerous and arrogant if it was just a human institution. But it is Christ who has kept the Church that he founded visible and united. His promises, and not just human efforts, have kept the Church faithful. His Spirit leads the Church, slowly but with assurance, towards all truth. His voice speaks infallibly in the Church's infallible teaching. His strength gives power to the Church and to all her members. The Catholic Church alone is the universal and guaranteed sign of Christ's presence in the world. It is not one denomination among many; it is the home of all Christians who have been unable to accept denominational Christianity, who believe that Christ is faithful to the Church that he founded and that this Church has continued through history.

This faith is the reason why the Catholic Church is so committed to ecumenism, to sharing its life with other

Christian communities, and to sharing in their life. There are tragic and painful differences between Christians; and Catholics refuse to obscure these. Yet Catholics are so concerned with unity and truth that nothing will stop them trying to discover and deepen their unity with other Christians. Their faith in Jesus Christ and in his Catholic Church is not a barrier to ecumenism; it is what gives them hope; it is what makes them want to share their faith, to share in the faith of others, and to work for unity.

What Catholics believe

All the gifts that belong to the Catholic Church are really only the expression of one simple thing - Jesus Christ. Nothing matters more than our union with him, our union with each other in him, and our being caught up in his life with the Father and the Holy Spirit. This is what holiness is; this is what life is about. The whole life of the Catholic Church is concerned with Christ, with bringing God's love and salvation to us. The Catholic Church is one because Christ is one, and he has given us this means of being united with him, of becoming a part of his body. The Catholic Church speaks authoritatively and infallibly because Christ speaks the truth to us, now as in the past. The Catholic Church gives us the sacraments and celebrates the Mass because in this way Christ's life and sacrifice are made real for us, right here, right now.

Every Catholic belief, however marginal, is simply another way of knowing Christ and what he means to us; every Catholic devotion, however obscure, is just another human way of loving Christ. If we think that the Catholic Church comes between Christ and his people then we have missed the point: Christ loves us through the Catholic Church. *He* loves us, *he* teaches us, *he* forgives us, *and he* makes us holy. We can't save ourselves; we can't defeat the terrible evil that exists in the world by ourselves. We need the Catholic Church because we need Jesus Christ, truly God and truly human. The Catholic Church is simply the way that he has chosen to be present in the world most clearly and surely.

By being drawn more and more into the life of the Catholic Church we fix our gaze more fully upon Christ, not less. This is the life of the angels and the saints. Mary, Jesus' mother, the mother of God, is the greatest of the saints. In her we see most clearly what the love of Christ has done for someone, and so we learn something about the Church. Her whole life was one big 'Yes' to the work of God's Spirit in her, her whole purpose was to love and to be loved by Christ. She brought him into the world, she cared for him and loved him unceasingly, she helped others to know and love him. Mary stood by him in his deepest and darkest moments, she offered her life in union with his on the cross, she took his closest disciple to be her son, she witnessed his resurrection from death, and with the apostles she received his Holy Spirit.

Without Mary's constant faithfulness, her passionate love, her unwavering hope, Christ would not have been given to the world. This is the role of the Catholic Church - not to exist for itself, but to bring Jesus Christ to the world, to be the sure and lasting presence of his truth, his sacrifice, his beauty, and his overwhelming love.

What can I do now?

If you would like to find out more about the Catholic Church, but are not sure what to do next, here are some ideas.

Read about the Catholic Church

Find out what the Church teaches. Get one of the many catechisms of Catholic belief that are available. Look at any collections of Catholic prayers that you can find. Read about the history of the Church. Read about the lives of the saints. At the end of this pamphlet I list a few books and websites that might be useful.

Talk to Catholics you know

Don't be afraid to ask Catholics you know about their faith and what it means to them. If you don't know who to talk to, get in touch with the priest at your nearest Catholic Church. He will be helpful and happy to talk. He will not pressure you to do or think anything that you don't want to. (His telephone number will be in the telephone directory under 'Catholic Churches'; or search for your local Catholic Church on the web).

Visit a Catholic Church

Look around it. Find out where the Blessed Sacrament is reserved and stay there in Christ's presence for a few minutes. (There is usually a red candle by the Blessed Sacrament.) Go to Mass if you can - the times of the Masses are usually printed on a notice board by the main door to the church.

Join an enquiry group at your local Catholic Church

Most parishes run meetings or talks for people who want to find out more about the Catholic faith. Ask your local parish priest about these. You might be nervous about going to a group, but there is always something positive about meeting with other people and sharing one's faith. It is good to realise that you are not alone in your search for the truth.

Pray

If you already pray regularly, pray especially that God will increase your faith. Pray that God will help you to know his Catholic Church more fully, that he will guide you and show you the truth. Pray that God will give you the strength to follow that truth.

If you don't pray regularly, then do try to. Nothing happens without prayer. Pray anytime, pray anywhere - pray right now if you can. Talk to God in your own words. If you don't know how to start, say slowly any prayers that you know off by heart, like the Lord's Prayer. It doesn't matter how self-conscious or stupid or empty you feel. It doesn't matter what terrible things you've done, or how little you believe in God. Start by asking him to help you to pray; say thank you for the good things in your life - however small; say sorry for the things you know you've done wrong; ask God to help you in all your needs, in all your difficulties; ask him to help those you love; tell him that you love him, that you trust him, even if you don't feel that you do; ask him to increase your faith.

Try to pray regularly, at least every day when you get up and when you go to bed, even if it's only for two minutes. More than anything else - be honest with God, he doesn't want us to pretend that we are someone else; he loves us just as we are.

If we pray, and if we try to do what we know is right, then God will give us everything that we need. He will guide us and bring us to share in his own glorious life, united with his Son Jesus Christ, in the unity of his Holy Spirit - now, in this world, and in the unending joy of heaven.

St Paul writes: 'Glory be to him whose power, working in us, can do infinitely more than we can ask or imagine; glory be to him from generation to generation in the Church and in Christ Jesus for ever and ever. Amen.' (*Ep* 3:20, 21)

Further reading and research

Compendium of the Catechism of the Catholic Church (London: Catholic Truth Society, 2006). [The Catholic Church's official shorter Catechism, in question and answer format. Also available online: search for the title]

Catechism of the Catholic Church, Revised Edition (London: Geoffrey Chapman, 1999). [The best guide to the official teaching of the Catholic Church. Also available online: search for the title]

David Albert Jones, *Christianity: An Introduction to the Catholic Faith* (Oxford: Family Publications, 1999). [Very good short pamphlet on the basics of the Catholic faith]

David Albert Jones, *Living Life to the Full: An Introduction to the Moral and Social Teaching of the Church* (Oxford: Family Publications, 2001). [Very good short pamphlet on the Church's moral teaching]

Alan Schreck, *Catholic and Christian* (Cincinnati, Ohio: Servant Books, 2004). [One of the best popular introductions to the Catholic faith. Not difficult to read]

Herbert McCabe, The Teaching of the Catholic Church: A New Catechism of Christian Doctrine (Darton, Longman and Todd: London, 2000). [Thought-provoking question and answer catechism]

Alban McCoy, *An Intelligent Person's Guide to Catholicism* (London and New York: Continuum, 2001). [Tries to answer the common questions that people ask about the Catholic faith. Based on talks to university students]

Roderick Strange, *The Catholic Faith* (London: Darton, Longman and Todd, 1996). [Excellent, thoughtful chapters on the basic Catholic beliefs. The author is very conscious of people's doubts and objections. Based on talks to university students]

George Weigel, *Letters to a Young Catholic* (Leominster: Gracewing, 2004). [A more imaginative way in to Catholic beliefs and principles. Full of stories and examples from Catholic lives]

Donald W. Wuerl and Ronald Lawler, eds., *The Teaching of Christ: A Catholic Catechism for Adults,* 5th ed. (Huntington, Indiana: Our Sunday Visitor, 2005). [One of the best and most comprehensive catechisms. Very clear. Full of references to the official Catechism of the Catholic Church]

Gerald O'Collins and Mario Farrugia, *Catholicism: The Story of Catholic Christianity* (Oxford: Oxford University Press, 2003). [A more demanding book, which is like a textbook of mainstream Catholic theology. Very valuable for those who want to go deeper to investigate the history and debates around Catholic thinking]

Most of these books can be ordered from your local bookshop or bought from an internet seller such as Amazon. There are many Catholic booksellers in the UK, some of which also sell through the internet. They have a good selection of Catholic books which you could browse through. Why not contact:

> The Catholic Truth Society
> 40-46 Harleyford Road
> Vauxhall, London, SE11 5AY
> Tel: 020 7640 0042
> http://www.cts-online.org.uk

> The Catholic Truth Society
> Bookshop
> 25a Ashley Place,
> Westminster Piazza
> Victoria, London
> Tel: 020 7834 3163

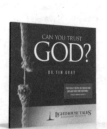

FORMED®
THE CATHOLIC FAITH.
ON DEMAND.

Discover the site that gathers more Catholic content in one place.

One convenient website
Save the time you used to spend searching and find the Catholic content you want. On demand and available when you are.

High quality
You'll always find beautiful, trustworthy, Catholic content.

New and updated regularly
Discover new and fresh materials every week.

More choices
Easily choose from a wide range of content options: movies, Ebooks, audio talks, and video studies.

Login to formed.org for a free 7-day trial.

CATHOLIC STUDY BIBLE APP

SCRIPTURE IN THE PALM OF YOUR HAND

The entire Catholic Bible (RSV-2CE) can be downloaded
for free! Packed with additional content from the Augustine
Institute, Ignatius Press, and other Catholic apostolates, this
app unlocks the beauty and richness of Scripture.

iPad iPhone
iPod touch   Google play   kindle fire

This incredible **free** app brings the Bible to life!

- Complete text of the Old and New Testaments (RSV-2CE)
- Truth & Life™ Dramatized Audio New Testament—
  free Gospel of John
- 10 hours of **free** audio commentary from Dr. Scott Hahn
- Over 140 Lighthouse Talks

**Download now by searching for Catholic Study Bible
in the App Store**